For Sharing With
/
None

June 2009

To my good friend
Bobby — without
whose *caring affection*
you and I would not
have the beauty and
comfort that surround us
and makes life good.

Love,
Mom

Fear, Trembling & Renewal

Poems to Age With

by Norma Roth

authorHOUSE®

AuthorHouse™
1663 Liberty Drive, Suite 200
Bloomington, IN 47403
www.authorhouse.com
Phone: 1-800-839-8640

© 2008 Norma Roth. All rights reserved.

No part of this book may be reproduced, stored in a retrieval system, or transmitted by any means without the written permission of the author.

First published by AuthorHouse 11/14/2008

ISBN: 978-1-4389-0460-3 (sc)

Printed in the United States of America
Bloomington, Indiana

This book is printed on acid-free paper.

Photographic art courtesy of Mike Jackman

Do not go gentle into that good night,
Old age should burn and rave at close of day:
Rage, rage against the dying of the light.

Do Not Go Gentle Into That Good Night... Dylan Thomas.

PROLOGUE TO FEAR, TREMBLING & RENEWAL:
poems for the mature

When the snow begins to fall...we know, it may be
the last best time, the snowflake with its many shapes,
no two alike, continues to intrigue us: colorless,
it is all color, tasteless, it can seem like the purest of water,
and when it touches our skin, it can feel as a soft caress –
yet, too, for those of us in our mature years, there is a
further metaphor to contend with: a season we may not be
ready for and cannot stop....

This book of poetry is a book for the mature: those
of us who are trying to face life as it is, feeling the
fear of getting older – the knowledge that one
doesn't have an age past this; the trembling of
wondering if we have yet spoken with the voice that
is truly ours – and if there is still time! And, if we
can get past the fear and trembling, the faint and
lingering hope that we can renew our dreams
and rededicate our lives and ourselves to be true
to the "selves" we want to be...until we are no
more.

I dedicate this book of poetry to renewal:

Come take my hand in yours
remember yourself, the self of dreams
renew those quests
temper them with wisdom (and maturity)
and take hold of the golden ring
and go with it...life may still have
those moments that are truly yours –
waiting...

Norma

TABLE OF CONTENTS

PROLOGUE: ESSAY: *POEMS FOR THE MATURE*   vii

I. FEAR

poems: *(fears)*

THEY DON'T SEE ME ANYMORE	1
THE SNOW BEGINS TO FALL	2
CHANGING LANDSCAPES	3
THE SPILL	4
BECOMING MY MOTHER	6
FEARS	7
IT TAKES TIME	8
INSULT	9
HOW RIDICULOUS TO BE 60	11
ANOTHER WORLD BECKONS	12
UNEXPECTED MOMENTS	14

> *they don't see me anymore...*
>   *they don't see me as I am*
>   *they see me only as I appear*
>   *slowing, greying, wrinkling*
>   *they used to glance and stay, now*
>   *a glance and a glance away*
>   *I used to get a smile and a wink*
>   *now only a quick look –*
>   *waiting to be discarded*
>   *I am now of the disregarded*
>   *why don't they see me as I was*
>   *as I know I am, as I feel I AM –*
>   *but they do not...and so I know*
>   *as they form the mirror to my soul*
>   *if I let them – I will be old...*
>   *and invisible*
>   *I am afraid.*

II. TREMBLING

poems: *(trembling)*

FRIENDS GONE	15
SNOW FILLS MY WORLD	16
SO THE MIND TURNS	17
ALMOST GONE	18
INTIMIDATION	19
SHATTERING BREAKDOWN	20
COLD WINTER SKY, PART I	21
I TREMBLE NOW	22
WINTER SUN, PART I	23
LAST LIGHT OF DAY	24

Cold sun through
steel-grey sky
sudden ray
strong light
remaining —
dizzying eyes
involuntary
closure —
eyes forced open
finding
light fading
sky lifeless
grey covering
closing off
last flickering
light...
I tremble.

(from Winter Sky)

III. RENEWAL

ESSAY: COMPANION POEMS: *RESPONSES TO FEAR & TREMBLING*	27

poems: *(reprieve)*

COMING OUT	28
REPRIEVE	29
COLD WINTER SKY, PART II	30
THEN AND NOW	31
AFTER THE SPILL	32
WINTER'S SUN, PART II	34
LAST FRENZIED DANCE	35
LAST LIGHT OF DAY, PART II	36
CLEAR THE COBWEBS	37
NEW BEGINNINGS	38
GRAB FOR THE RING	39
DO I DARE	41

'Do I dare?' Mr. Eliot
(I have thought long on this):
YES, I dare!
I will not settle for Hamlet's servant
That will not do…
I will be Hamlet (or his sister) or – perhaps
nothing – but at least I will try
with my every breath –
'I grow old…' so 'I grow old…'
I will still say yes to life
thrust my fears to the wildest winds
swirl and spin and spit
as long as there is a spark…

(from: Do I Dare)

RENEWAL continued...

poems: *(epiphanies and flashes)*

SYMPHONY-CACOPHONY	43
RENEWAL	44
I HAVE THINGS TO DO	45
RE-AWAKENING	46
A GOOD LIFE	47
UNCHANGED	48
FLOWERING TREES	49
STILLNESS & MY WORLD	52
THE REST OF MY LIFE	54
SEIZE THE MOMENT	57
SATISFACTION	58

life is a cycle...my life cycle
none the better, none the worse
life – my life – is what I make it
after all:
I am the artist
I carve my world –
I will not sleep until
the last breath is drawn
I will not succumb:
greatness may be before
not behind – I will not judge why...
I will live!

RENEWAL continued...

poems: *(postscript: sharing renewal)*

EVERY YEAR THEN	59
MIRROR, MIRROR ON THE WALL	60
LIKE THE WIND	62
GREY PEBBLE BEACH	64
I CAN GROW OLD HERE	65

*I can grow old here where
there is no time...there is only all time
where life is as it has always been – as
it was yesterday, is today, and will be
tomorrow – and were it to change, it
would still be the same...*

(from I Can Grow Old Here)

Epilogue:

ESSAY: *TIME TO MOVE ON*	67

poems:

STILL THERE IS MAGIC	68
TIME TO MOVE ON	69
THESE ARE THE MOMENTS OF MY LIFE	70

*Time to move on...
we may have moments
only moments
but oh, the glory of those
moments that are the
splendor of "my" life....*

(from Time to Move On...)

FEAR

they don't see me anymore...
    they don't see me as I am
    they see me only as I appear
    slowing, greying, wrinkling
    they used to glance and stay, now
    a glance and a glance away
    I used to get a smile and a wink
    now only a quick look –
    waiting to be discarded
    I am now of the disregarded
    why don't they see me as I was
    as I know I am, as I feel I AM –
    but they do not...and so I know
    as they form the mirror to my soul
    if I let them – I will be old...
            and invisible
            I am afraid.

THE SNOW BEGINS TO FALL...

The snow begins to fall
I fall slightly, too, but perhaps
it is only a tremor
a way to see the world
anew – old, grey, dismal
but with specks of white
How is it that little dots
before our eyes can change vision?

CHANGING LANDSCAPE

mind
not yet in gear
struggling to meet
day
in a new way

yet not
quite new
as old
struggles
to be
enfolded
in new

memories of
former times
not quite
done
flash back
flash forward
seeking space

go back
go forward
go on
it's okay
mind struggling
to meet
day

new way
not necessarily
better, maybe
even the lesser
I fear it.

THE SPILL

All in order
arranged perfectly
for my needs and senses

A cup of strong coffee
freshly roasted
a new book

Ah, inhale that fragrance
as I sit
so comfortably

turning a crisp page
sipping a cup of aromatic
roast...

And then – THE SPILL...
The spill: fallen
from newly fragile fingers

stains of freshly brewed coffee
spreading over the freshly
laundered pristine cloth

placed so carefully on the table
spreading over all
like a rushing river

in early spring, flowing
over everything in its path
covering all with slimy brown.

Is this, then, dreaded old age?
The moment when
all begins to unravel
like a ball of yarn fallen
from once sturdy hands
unraveling on and on...

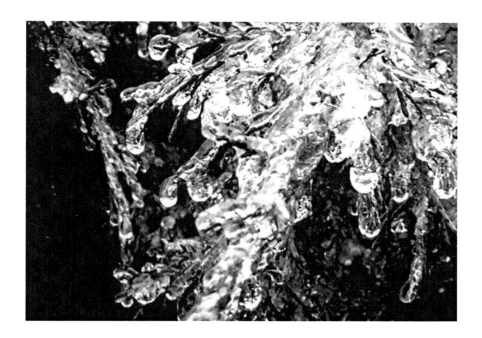

BECOMING MY MOTHER

In strange ways
and place
In strange times
and phases
I look in the mirror
and see my mother:
I comb my hair
my mother is there

I look at my form
she is there
I hear my phrases
they are hers
where ever I am
where ever I go
whatever I do
she is there

Have I become her?
Have we become one?

I had thought
somewhere in between
being and becoming
I would become
something other
uniquely mine
myself and no other
was I mistaken?
have I merely repeated
the cycle now closing?

Have I become her?
Have we become one?

FEARS

In dreams
my youth is there
awake
my mother's age
is mine.

IT TAKES TIME

It takes time
    to prepare
for the rest of a life

    Do I have it?

It takes patience
    to unfold goals
for the rest of a life

    Do I have it?

It takes strength
    to make decisions
for the remaining years

    Of a life.

INSULT

An insurance company had the nerve
to send me a birthday card
reminding me – stating it in print –
that the number 59 was turning to 60!

A nasty and venomous act
disguised so carelessly
a number meaningless before
now a marker not to be ignored

I fully understand
what they are trying to say
no longer a part of youth
certainly past motherhood

the old crone stage...
remembered from fairy tales
past even middle age
and entering the forbidden zone
which comes before...

The nerve to remind me –
It reminds me of long ago,
I asked my mentor and friend
What it felt like to be 60:

"Why," she replied sadly:
"I still look out at the world
with the eyes of 23." Later,
on the eve of his birthday

a dear friend remarked:
"How," I wonder "does
a 30 year old get trapped
in the body of a man who is 60?"

Does the insurance company think
when they send out these cheerful notes
that remind me of a corner turned –
how saddened that might make me?

HOW RIDICULOUS TO BE 60...

How ridiculous to be 60
   when I still remember
   my mother bathing and feeding me
   her hands embracing and soothing
   her food healing.

How absurd to be 65
   when I still remember
   my mother holding my hand
   as we walked crossing streets
   her hands both strong and tender
   her love unalterable and forever.

And when I am 75:
   will my mother still walk with me
   along the river banks of the Charles?
   will we stand under the cherry blossoms
   in May as we did when I graduated at 30
   and we were all so proud?

ANOTHER WORLD

In the midst of the simple task
washing my hands
I had washed away age –
Suddenly I saw a
younger hand:
the hand was as pure
as a bar of soap
smooth, unlined
not a trace of
wrinkle or roughness
appeared.

Strange thing
mind returned to
other days – and I
saw the young child
standing at a bathroom
vintage of another
place and time
only for me at this
moment it was
that time – I was that
child.

If old age be this
Will I mind?
Those were such
lovely days, when
all the needs of the
young child were
taken care of by
a nurturing mother
and I was kissed
each night and tucked
in as though, indeed
I was a princess in a fairy tale....

UNEXPECTED MOMENTS

I watch as the sunlight streams in
through windows everywhere
through drapes and slats
through every niche and crevice round...
no crack can hold it back.

Room ablaze: brilliant rays warming
absorbing, luring me towards dreams –
eyes close drifting criss-cross currents
move swiftly through my being
reaching a core...I slumber.

Awakening to sun almost gone
quickly departing day, greying sky
closure suddenly strikes deep within
sadness, tears well, wonder...
such quiet sudden – unexpected ends.

TREMBLING

friends gone
        lovers lost in other loves
        what was it I dreamed?
        in the long ago
        or was it only yesterday
        I reached out my hand
        to worlds that beckoned
        bright, light, warm
        but that was so long ago
        I tremble...

SNOW FILLS MY WORLD

My world fills with snow –
Am I ready?
strange, sensuous, seductive
flecks seemingly from nowhere
shapes seemingly from nothing
touch almost tender from...

momentary image:
snow flakes falling...falling on me
pain less – promise of peace
bringing suffering to an end
silence, sleep, seductive snow –
Am I ready?

Why do I tremble?

SO, THE MIND TURNS

So, the mind turns, miles away
so many, all else disappears
entering and walking
along a path – of yesteryear

reliving a moment, a memory…

Seated in a room, small
surrounded by
rays of today, the mind drifts
to another room, and another

lost in a thought – loved…

great images, chosen carefully
moments divine, lingering
longingly in yesterday –
hard choice coming back

yesterday's lives and loves were better…

Reliving cherished moments –
no longer memories
vivid, strong, good, near
no longer memories

becoming more real than today.

ALMOST GONE

Almost gone
trees bare
a few leaves
remaining
brown, burnt orange
lying silent
trembling to the touch.

Enough time
before thoughts dry
before senses fail
experience diminish
motivation wanes
mind empties
time ends?

INTIMIDATION

shock waves
dart through body
what was that?

smile
fog drops
body rigid
words fractured:

I thought I did
did didnot did

seek cover
sifting sand
layers of my mind
question

soul screaming
try a correction
silence
shout

head silent
soul whimpers
heart hurts

Surrender

SHATTERING BREAKDOWN

Shattering breakdown of nerve endings
plunge sideways morose uncertainty

torture chamber of unfulfilled dreams
invasion of body atoms, protons, nano particles

at this juncture of life
at this limitation of space

density of fog so fearful
a tiny misstep can become

the "leap into the void"
I may not be able to stop.

COLD WINTER SKY, Part I

Cold sun through
steel-grey sky
sudden ray
strong light
remaining –
dizzying eyes
involuntary
closure –
eyes forced open
finding
light fading
sky lifeless
grey covering
closing off
last flickering
light...
I tremble.

I TREMBLE NOW

friends gone
lovers lost in other loves
what was it I dreamed
in the long ago

Or was it only yesterday
I reached out my hand
to worlds that beckoned
bright, light, warm –

did I dream it?
did I see it?
do I want it still?
can I reach out?
My hand trembles

friends gone
lovers lost in other loves –
or not remembered –
dreams unfulfilled…
I tremble

WINTER'S SUN   Part I

Sunlight falls upon me through windows
quickly I run to close the slats, draw the drapes
before the sun's light can reach me

its rays penetrate too deeply:
danger lies in those radiant rays —
sharp penetration of a thunderbolt hurled

I have learned to turn from the sun's light
before it can bring harm to me:
those radial beams so intense lie in wait

for those who are not careful
I have learned to keep strict watch for them
trembling, I pull the drapes closed.

LAST LIGHT OF DAY

Last light of day streaming through my window
everything contained within this room:
joy, calmness, hope, love, beauty, laughter
photos in elegant frames by the mantle piece
count time that is done –
frames waiting in wrappings surrounding the
floors of my closet count time not yet had –
those faces in those frames reflect all at our best:
shining with incandescence.

Coolness drifts slowly into my room
through cracks in the window
shedding a cold grey light over all
last rays of light flicker in though my window
everything contained here that is my life:
beauty, calmness, hope …tears, sadness, despair
I feel a chill and take refuge beneath my oversize quilt
I am getting old…I fear what tomorrow may bring

Suddenly, I am trembling –I burrow deeper into
the heavy velvet fabrics of my quilt seeking protection:
I seek darkness to block out memories
I seek comfort to last through the day and into night
If I stay here long enough, perhaps…
the trembling and fear may disappear.

RENEWAL

- **reprieve**

- **epiphanies & flashes**

- **postscript**

ESSAY: COMPANION POEMS: RESPONSES TO FEAR AND TREMBLING:

COLD WINTER SKY, Part II
AFTER THE SPILL
WINTER SUN, Part II
LAST FRENZIED DANCE
LAST LIGHT OF DAY

In this section, readers will find a set of companion pieces that form an important layer of text. An unusual section but not a unique one: long ago when Christopher Marlow wrote his well known verse: *Come live with me and be my love and we will all the pleasures prove....* Sir Walter Raleigh, a while later, took it upon himself to respond with these conditions: *If all the world were young and truth in every shepherd's tongue... could youth last, and love still breed, Had joy no date, nor age no need....* Thus, a trend of poets speaking to each other through verse and throughout the ages – and thus speaking to us – from different vantage points.

I have adopted a variation of this: here it is I who respond to pieces written in an earlier section of this book taking a different tone and mood to earlier statements – that is, taking exception to some of the fears and trembling of the earlier poems.

So, *The Spill* which gives rise to the seemingly first signs of the coming of that "no rebound moment" of age is followed by *After The Spill* which looks at the coffee spilled, the book pages curling, the pristine tablecloth browning and asserts: *you can wipe it up, can't you...* adding a reassuring thought; and while earlier *Winter Sun* describes our society's strict adherence to closing out that dangerous sunlight that sees us drawing our drapes, *Winter Sun,* Part II lingers longingly over the ability of that sun to provide warmth to the heart and soul, positing: *it is winter's sun after all...*and besides: *the sun and I have been friends too long to part now...* And so it goes...

Norma

reprieve

COMING OUT

      wrapped
cocoon like
I dare not move
instead I allow
warmth to seep
through the many
layers and textures
until the warmth
penetrates the interior
      that is me.

REPRIEVE

It's okay, snow has come
and with it light!

I forgot
how snow's white
replaces dark night

dancing on trees
enhancing the leaves

filling dark crevices
of earth with white

I forgot
how snow bright
replaces dark night

such intensity
there is no night.

COLD WINTER SKY, Part II

Unbelievable:
cold sun through
blue-grey sky
sudden ray
strong light
paining – yet
dazzling eyes
involuntary closure
followed quickly
by desire
to see – to know
eyes open
finding
light fading
sky quieting
grey covering
closing off
last flickering
light
sad, yet
strangely
soothing
–maybe even
exciting –
After all,
    IT IS LIGHT!

Companion piece to Cold Winter Sky (*Fears*)

THEN AND NOW

Between the raindrops
  and a birth of
  buds and babies
  I exist

Between seasons passing
  moments of
  time stolen
  I exist

Between a chore
  and a thought
  baby talk and a walk
  I exist.

Between a pain
  and a moment of light
  reflection and excitement
  I exist

Between a sleep
  moments of doubt, confusion
  haze and clarity
  I exist

Betweeen dying cells
  and trembling fears
  darkness and light
  I exist...

    I EXIST!

        (dedicated to T.S. Eliot)

AFTER THE SPILL

So, the coffee spilled
the book pages curled back
the tablecloth stained...

Well, then, we'll just do it again:
wipe up that stupid spill
test the paper towels

see if they really
do the job
they are meant to do

gently sop up the coffee
from the recent new book
perhaps still readable

wash off the table
before the stain
darkens the wood

underneath the pristine
cloth now
soaking in soapy water.

Put it back in order:
you can do that!
the years must teach something

There – it is done:
pour another cup of coffee
not quite the same

sit at the less than perfect table
let the book dry
taste the coffee tinged with age

perhaps this is more suitable
after all...
Life beckons

Companion piece to Spill (*Fears*)

WINTER'S SUN, Part II

Sunlight shines on me through windows
bright – rays penetrate my body
radiant warmth fills me

It is only winter's sun, after all –
those lovely rays –

warming, seducing – welcoming me
granting me a moment of peace
from the cold grey metal of winter.

It is only winter's sun, after all –
those lovely rays –

Surely something that feels so good
cannot be other-to need
protection for me

The sun and I have been
friends too long to part now
I will brave it.

Companion Piece to "Winter Sun," (*Trembling*)

LAST FRENZIED DANCE

But wait...
the wind comes...
    blustery, howling, blowing
    lingering brown, burnt orange leaves
    free themselves from beneath the first snow
    shaking off their winter white cover
    they swirl and twirl in rhythmic pattern
    blown higher and higher freer and freer
    twirling and swirling in almost devilish symphony
    perhaps — yes — there is still time for
    the final, frantic, frenzied best dance....

Companion Piece to "Almost Gone" (*Trembling*)

LAST LIGHT OF DAY, Part II

A sudden ray of warmth penetrates me
from an unknown source –it cannot be winter's light
but rather a warmth deep within the interior
of my being like a gentle wave winding through
the pulses filling my arteries and veins with a comfort
that has long been lacking; carrying me away
from the darkness that has been finding such a
welcome place of habitation within my soul:
the waves seem to be gathering force
driving out the darkness like the pulse of the moon
pushing waves onto the beach with such force
one dare not breathe.

Deep within the core that is me, I embrace the pulse
that is seeping into the passageways of my body
and soul, momentarily returning a tranquillity that tastes
like cool water on a summer day –
I peek out and dare to move up from and out of
what once, I thought was peaceful protection…
The pictures on the mantle piece suddenly take on
a transcendence: different hues of color
dancing flecks of gold – they seem lit from within
now luminescent: I reach out to touch them tenderly –

tomorrow, perhaps I will look past this fear and trembling
tomorrow, perhaps, I will once again look for the light
                                        to guide my way…

Companion Piece, Last Light of Day (*Trembling*)

CLEAR THE COBWEBS

Clear the cobwebs
know you should
layer after layer
dust it off

dust with care

there may be
worlds waiting there
parts untouched
parts of you

dust with care

NEW BEGINNINGS

Open to:
discovery
potential
the new
the almost
discarded
the epiphany

Set forth
on new
journeys
half started
never started
always there
revealed once more

Dust off
treasures
hidden from view
but not from mind
and soul
longing to become
ready to burst out –

Let the body
fill:
with joy
exhilaration
excitement
pleasure extremis –
fog lifting
accept

Life...

GRAB FOR THE RING

Loosen the straps
peek around the corner
tiptoe, take a look – not too long
dare...Be daring!
What do you have to lose?

Grab for the ring...

It may be gold, Yes!
or more likely brass –
maybe merely gold dust
or simply dust –
disappointed?
frustrated?

not as much as when
your hair was raven
and turned to grey.

Life is like that
drifts and drafts –
winds and gusts –
snow and sleet –
snags and falls...

Grab hold hard:

nothing ventured,
nothing gained
so the saying goes
Between the idea
And the reality...
Falls the Shadow

but hasn't it always ?

Still, you may be the
one to grab the golden ring
take the road less traveled
see where it leads this time –

last time you played it safe
didn't you? maybe bought
into other people's plans –
life may be best lived by
those who dare
What do you have to lose?

Grab for the ring!

Go ahead, glance down that
other road – less to lose
take it without expectation
merely for the ride
because you want to
regardless of where it lets you off

because it is your life
because it is the last of life
because, life is…

DO I DARE?

'Do I dare?' Mr. Eliot
(I have thought long on this):
YES, I dare!
I will not settle for Hamlet's servant
That will not do...
I will be Hamlet (or his sister) or – perhaps
nothing – but at least I will try
with my every breath
'I grow old...' so 'I grow old...'
I will still say yes to life
thrust my fears to the wildest winds
swirl and spin and spit
as long as there is a spark...
I will do it...I may not do it all
but I can try –
life is in the trying
life...is in the trying.

Response to A Thought: *The Love Song of J. Alfred Prufrock*. T.S. Eliot

epiphanies & flashes

Past, present and future
merge in a symphony —
perhaps merely a   cacophony
of sound and non - sound
But:
I am the artist
I carve my world
time is mine.

RENEWAL

The snow has thawed
Spring is here
flowers in bloom
everywhere...
a chance for renewal
a chance for me

Winter, Spring, Summer, Fall
these are the cycles of
my life
these are the seasons
of my heart...
I will live them all

The snow has thawed
Spring is here
flowers in bloom
everywhere...
a chance for renewal
a chance for me

Summer will come
after, Fall --
and Winter – then Spring
may come once more...
these are the seasons
of my life –
I will live them all.

I HAVE THINGS TO DO!

I have things to do
songs to sing
poems to write
photographs to take
life to live...

the photo will be of ice
frozen white, cold
yet beautiful –
exquisite delicate form
and shape

the poem will be of
infinite possibilities
fulfillment of promises
and potential long known
and yet to know...

the song will be of tones
and melodies collected
over a lifetime, known
to me from other sources
and those not yet known

the song will be of myself
the poems will be of my heart
the photographs of my choice
the life to live ... mine.

I have things to do...

RE- AWAKENING

Awakening to the light of a brand new
day – knowing this day is different, unique,
special, maybe splendid but not why? Poking
around the squeaky door held open just a
notch by the slippers being sought, deciding
not to intrude upon the comfort I sense in the
slipper holding the doorway open just
wide enough for one to slip through, I turn sideways
pleased as I make my way through the sleeping room
into the awaiting outer room awash with
the early morning light. Remembering too–
from another time how bare feet could feel on surfaces
I gingerly touch the still cool wooden floor
warmed a bit by the early rays casting light and feel
the delicious coolness from my toes clear through
to the limbs and into the core that is me. I glance outside
and wonder if my giant Sycamore feels as I do
 – sun's early rays striking at its core moving quickly towards
its limbs. Quiet as a kitten, newly awakened,
I stretch to let the light in….

A GOOD LIFE

A walk along the river
   gathering flowers
    feeling wind
      hearing water

Senses coming alive
   limbs intact
    mind alert
     life good

Alert
  to sound
   to nature
    to feeling

  – to Life!

UNCHANGED

The beautiful silence of a room
the magnificence of the sun setting
the harmony and tranquility of musical
notes floating through the air
the sensations of warmth, wind and water
soothing, satisfying, transcending
sitting in a quiet place contemplating:
these things remain unchanged.

FLOWERING TREES
Waiting To Be Noticed

No one seems to notice
the flowers on the trees:

For years I have rushed
out to see them –

one has to move quickly
they flower for so few

moments... yet their
magnificence is

like the continued sparkle
of that first diamond ring

like the exhilaration upon
watching a golden sunset

This year the flowering trees
seem particularly sensuous

their delicate velvet petals
herald Spring:

their look like orchids
waiting to be touched.

I have decided they are more
beautiful than Spring flowers

coming when I can't wait for Spring
rushing to greet me –

So many people do not even notice
those tiny buds that flower on trees

clusters of form and elegance
and absolute moments of perfection

This year the buds seem to be
remaining longer than in past years

do they linger because
I am there with them

or is it that I go to
watch them every day?

do they seem to endure
because they know

I will catch them as they fall
and take some home with me

to press their petals in a book
small tiny flowers

to remind me such
short lives bring Spring's

first burst of passion and glory
that early burst of beauty

that may last long if one holds them
in one's heart – and looks at

their petals in a book for the
rest of a life.

STILLNESS AND MY WORLD

The stillness haunts me
I look at a painting
capturing
oneness of
sky with sea
The artist's easel
at her best:

muted shades
pink, blue, grey
mirror images
I look to the sea
contrasts and harmonies
blends, turns
upside downs
all into one

on the shore
artistic splashes
dark greens
shading landscape.
I put down the
easel of my mind

I leave the pen –
to walk into
the quieter landscape
absorbing into myself
the colors in the pallet
of my mind's eye.

The harmonious landscape
captures me:
I may decide to stay...

or – having imbibed
the stillness for awhile
I may wait ... returning
a later day

I am the artist;
I carve my world.

THE REST OF MY LIFE
Light By the River

I
"The light is so beautiful," she said
"I will walk around later"

"Don't make it too much later," he replied
"This is the shortest day of the year."

Quickly dressing, pulling on all the
lovely warmth from long ago,
she raced out from the house.

As the loveliness of the day and the
beauty of the light filled her senses,
she scolded herself for not being out of doors sooner

but, the unusual warmth of a late Fall day
and the prospect of sharing it lightened her life

without a moment's thought, her feet headed
down to the river by the perambulating streets

which she knew so well from nigh on 30 years
she was, after all, just following the light.

Knowing that the sun would set
soon, very soon—she started to run.

II
Before her, from the last small hill lay the river bare
the light from the sinking sun visibly shone on it

"Have I missed the last light?" she quietly asked
I couldn't have – not here – here there is always light

She breathed deeply as the sun seemed to peek through
the trees from the other side of the river

Yes it was setting, but it seemed to be waiting
for strollers like her—or maybe just for her.

Daringly, she looked directly at the setting sun
risking the onslaught of migraine pain

the rays moved through her like bullets
small pain for such pleasure, she thought

choosing to ignore it as
she moved silently to her bench

to watch the unfolding of the setting of the sun
the bench occupied she turned to her old friend

the giant aging Sequoia, it's huge hollow carved in
more than enough to fit her entire frame

though larger in contour than when she first came:
she spread her body and leaned into the waiting curvature

of the tree: she had a first rate seat to eternity.

III
"This is the first day of the rest of my life,"
the words echoed in her head moving quickly to her heart

she rested in the comfort of the tree whose
bare branches were but extensions of her limbs.

A spectacular show unfolding there by the river's edge
for those who had made their way here

the bikers, the runners, the strollers, the sitters
now silhouetted against the sky a single scull gliding by

She saw the show before her not once but twice
having learned long ago to don rose tinted glasses

that rendered the early golden sky a strong golden pink:
she now took them off to watch it all again.

She liked the strength of the vibrant colors best
time had been good to her down by the river these many years.

She basked in the golden light, now
turning orange and purple, moving to cover every space

covering her too; fulfillment embraced her for all she was
and maybe, too, for what was left for her to become.

SEIZE THE MOMENT

Today seems the day...
Energized without end
I feel I can do it all...

If only the day is long enough

My head teems with
Endless possibilities
I think I can do them all...

If only the day is long enough...

SATISFACTION

I laugh at myself
feeling good
thoughts coming
in such profusion
I can scarcely breathe

without a new one,
or old, tumbling
in on one another
clear as glass
sweet as the first kiss

I laugh again
almost a giggle,
knowing it will
not last
but happy enough
it has come

postscript

lives are lived in phases...this postscript shares some events from a life being lived in renewal.

>Every year, then...
>>a chance for
>>renewal
>>every year, then
>>flowers grow:
>>I can grow too.
>>Every year, then...
>>a new time
>>to be me.

MIRROR MIRROR ON THE WALL

One of those mornings to
stay in bed,
to arise slowly and watch
beginnings of changing
landscape in December
shuffling along in slippers
and still in night attire
making my way through
the morning looking
forward to night

Deciding to pull
some clothes on:
I will not stay ready for
night the whole day or
what is left of it

One glance in the mirror
that resides on the wall
it can hardly be a mistake
in my room so small
why bother…habit calls –

Well, just one glance…
Oh, my, *I look just fine*
my long curly locks
not yet touched
seems to frame
my face flatteringly

just enough to hide
what I do not want shown
just enough to show
the green from
my hazel hybrid eyes
stand out strong

strange, my bed attire, too,
looks somewhat appealing –
*maybe I should leave it
and go do this thing
that has been churning in
my mind—and will not let go* –

the dress suited to the task
the gown warm with purple
flowers across the bodice
draping in a lovely manner
beneath the soft robe
my body flowing gracefully
hiding all flaws – imagined
and otherwise – within
its dainty ruffled bodice
adding a touch of loveliness

yes, *I shall go and, perhaps
carpe diem –
seize the day
from myself
and my foolishness.*
mirror mirror on the wall
thank you for showing
me this day
the fairest of them all.

LIKE THE WIND

Here in the mountains
the wind is supreme
no one dares defy it...
It comes and goes
exactly as it pleases
pleasing no one but itself

When I hear the wind
I rush to the door
to let it in
I want to feel it on my face
I want it to surround me
with its coolness and freshness —

Sometimes when I get there
the wind has gone
it has become, in an instant
strangely quiet
silence greets me
I cannot find the wind

When I hear it again
I rush to the window and listen:
Sometimes I can hear its power
it never sounds the same:
it seems to take its power
from where it is, or
where it moves to and through

The creak of a house
it creeps into; the sound of chimes
it causes to play; the howling of trees
it bends to its will; the swish of the
leaves it blows down and around and
round in a diurnal swirl

How can something
so furious not be heard?
How can something
so masterful not be seen?
How can something with
such force not truly be known?

I am like the wind....

GREY PEBBLE BEACH

Standing on a grey pebble beach
more in keeping with the newer
phase of uncertainty
unnecessary baggage easy discard
other things lie abandoned too
on this grey pebbled beach
or discarded themselves somewhere
along the way – between life's
truth and reality –
Here standing on this pebble beach
natural forms surround

colors and hues of grey rust shed
accurate reflection of the scene,
the match striking: grey strands of hair
pushing through the once raven-haired
grey-blue of fading dungarees
outworn their day, but blending in better
with grey pebbles, blue-grey water
some softer colors, pinks, some greens
suggesting the sedateness more in
keeping with the inner life image I seek
Here standing on this grey pebble beach
I feel more at peace

I think I will spend more time here
the inner and outer reflect
a harmony truth and reality:
subtle manageable pebble greys
face, form life loss--
part of all that I am, seen
maybe all I can be--maybe not
other secrets may yet lie in wait for me
ready to be discovered amidst the natural
forms and uncertainties that are now my life.

I CAN GROW OLD HERE

There is a timelessness I feel in this place:
a quiet murmur of conversations
hands poised for poignant phrases
heads nodding in reminiscence and agreement
secrets and philosophy shared
sometimes overheard....

There is a sense of time lived
and time to come here
friends and lovers, hand in hand, walk paths
worn over by footsteps as I have done
seeing, sensing, dreaming, becoming...
being all that they are or can be...
untroubled by the universe.

I have a sense that I can live here forever –
whatever that might be for me –
this place encompasses all times:
youth, age and all the rest –
the seasons of life and the seasons of my life:
my eyes can see as they have always seen;
my hands clasp as they have always done
and I love as I have done before and can again.

I can see living here, when it is
as it has always been, as it was yesterday
today – and will be tomorrow
and even were it to change – it would be the same:
for there is no age when one looks
through the same eyes; there is no time when
one senses with the same passion;
and there is no change when one holds the hands
of a friend or a lover and looks on the world together....

Epilogue

*Every day then a new beginning
every day a new opportunity
to move closer to the you
that you know you want to be.*

*Within the self, there are other selves waiting
to be explored...this is the time to move on...*

STILL THERE IS MAGIC

Still there is magic:
let life absorb you
for a timeless moment
endless time...
put your foot
delicately into
the magic of the sea
open your arms wide
let your eyes scan
across the endless horizon
let life speak to you...

TIME TO MOVE ON

Within the self there are other selves
waiting to be explored:
they may not be the ones of childhood
they may not be the ones of adolescence
they may not be the ones of adulthood
but they are mine.

This is the time to move on...
past fear and trembling to world's renewal
the seasons move rapidly in the mountains
where I have spent so much time
I have learned one cannot linger too long
over the past, or the present will be gone.

Already the Fall is going – time to catch
a few leaves – Soon Winter will come...and soon
Winter will go...And then Spring may
come again.

THESE ARE THE MOMENTS OF MY LIFE

All things move in
   like lightning

a momentary light
   then gone, but...

Oh – the splendor
   of that moment

All things intensified
   the height

of splendor and beauty;
   the radiance

of the day at its
   most magnificent

Summer into Fall
   Winter, Spring

which has my destiny
   after all?

I care not as long as
   it is bountiful

and I take part in
  carving that destiny

and keep those splendid
  moments and memories
that are my life.

ABOUT THE AUTHOR

Norma Roth is an attorney, educator and individual scholar who has written poetry all her life. None has given her more sense of accomplishment than this present volume *Fear, Trembling & Renewal*: a collection of poems for the mature written over the last decade from her personal perspective and dedication to the last phase of a life – which she sees as a renewal. Ms. Roth is currently working on a companion piece, a book, *Aging With Grace, Dignity and Integrity Intact* subtitled: *Aging Defiantly!* slated for publication in the spring. Other publications include: *Scenes From A Summer Home: The House that Waited & Other Poems*; and *War: We Always Lose*. Several poems from the collection of war poems have received broad recognition, including Editor's Choice Award, and publication in *Centres of Expression* by Noble House; *The Best Poems and Poets of 2007* and *The International Library of Poetry Recognition Collection*.

> *Grow old along with me!*
> *The best is yet to be,*
> *the last of life, for which the*
> *first was made....*
>
> *Pippa Passes* by Robert Browning

Ms. Roth resides in Cambridge, MA and spends a great deal of time in the mountains of New Hampshire and the beautiful northern neighbor, Canada.

Printed in the United States
207567BV00001B/55-156/P